John Marshall

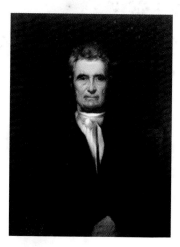

by
Stuart A. Kallen

Visit us at
www.abdopub.com

Published by ABDO Publishing Company, 4940 Viking Drive, Edina, MN 55435. Copyright ©2001 by Abdo Consulting Group, Inc. International copyrights reserved in all countries. No part of this book may be reproduced in any form without written permission from the publisher.

Printed in the United States.

Graphic design: John Hamilton
Cover Design: Maclean Tuminelly

Cover photos: Corbis
Interior photos and illustrations:
    AP/Wide World: p. 27
    Corbis: p. 5, 7, 9, 11, 13, 22, 29, 31, 33, 41, 45, 47, 51, 53, 55, 57, 59
    North Wind Picture Archives: p. 15, 17, 19, 21, 35, 37, 43
    Swem Library, College of William & Mary, p. 24, 25

Library of Congress Cataloging-in-Publication Data

Kallen, Stuart A., 1955-
    John Marshall / Stuart Kallen.
        p. cm. — (The Founding fathers)
    Includes index.
    Summary: A biography of the Chief Justice of the Supreme Court whose many decisions shaped American law and had lasting effects.
    ISBN 1-57765-016-6
    1. Marshall, John, 1755-1835—Juvenile literature.
2. Judges—United States—Biography—Juvenile literature.
3. United States. Supreme Court—Biography—Juvenile literature. [1. Marshall, John, 1755-1835. 2. Judges.
3. United States. Supreme Court—Biography.] I. Title.

KF8745.M3 K35 2001
347.73'2634—dc21
    [B]
                                                    98-005176

Contents

Introduction

A large mob of people crowded around the Federal Court Building in Richmond, Virginia. The press was out in full force. Politicians delivered solemn statements to anyone who would listen. Average citizens looked around for a glance at the rich and famous. In the courthouse, the most exciting trial of the day was taking place. The year was 1807, and Aaron Burr, a former vice president of the United States, was on the stand. Burr was charged with treason.

Like a modern celebrity trial, Burr had a stunning array of lawyers to defend him. President Thomas Jefferson created a stir by announcing Burr guilty even before the trial. And it was hard to find objective jury members; people who had not already made up their minds as to whether Burr was innocent or guilty.

The judge running the trial was John Marshall—Chief Justice of the United States Supreme Court. Marshall strongly disliked Burr, however, the judge was determined to see that Burr received justice amid the political fireworks.

Facing page: Chief Justice John Marshall.

The trial ended when the jury found Burr "not guilty" after only 30 minutes of deliberation. The press howled. The president called for Marshall's head. Politicians threatened to change the Constitution so this could never happen again. But John Marshall knew that Burr was innocent. Marshall put his own reputation on the line to be sure a fair trail was conducted in his courtroom. The publicity and public opinion did nothing to sway the judge.

John Marshall would sit as Chief Justice of the Supreme Court until 1835. His many decisions have shaped American law to this very day. But Marshall was more than a judge. He was a soldier, a patriot, and a fighter for Native American rights. From a log cabin in Virginia to the highest court in the land, John Marshall was an outstanding judge and an American patriot.

Former Vice President Aaron Burr was charged with treason.

Growing Up in Virginia

JOHN MARSHALL WAS ONE of the most respected Supreme Court Justices. Those who knew him often remarked at his humble beginnings. Marshall was born in a log cabin in Germantown, Virginia, on September 24, 1755. The cabin was in Virginia's backwoods, miles away from the nearest neighbor, but John wasn't lonely. He was the oldest of 15 children—eight brothers and six sisters.

Although the Marshalls lived in a cabin, they were not poor. John's father, Thomas, was a surveyor. So was the Marshalls' neighbor, George Washington. And like Washington, Thomas Marshall met many of Virginia's rich and powerful men through his job. Thomas Marshall was also a lawmaker in the House of Burgesses, the law-making body of Virginia.

A log cabin set in the mountains of rural Virginia.

Unlike many women of the time, John's mother Mary was able to read and write. She taught basic education to her large brood of children. Later a Scottish minister lived with the Marshalls and taught the children. By the time John was 12, he could read and speak Latin.

When he was 18, John decided he wanted to be a lawyer. In those days it was common practice for a young man to learn law by working with a practicing attorney. John worked with a local lawyer who worked 10 miles from his home. John walked the distance every day on foot.

John, however, had trouble thinking about his legal studies. The British ruled Virginia and the other American colonies at the time. When John was 18, he knew a war between England and America was coming soon. He wanted to join the fight.

Fighting in Norfolk

AMERICAN COLONISTS had been clashing with the British government for some time. When the English imposed taxes on the Americans, the colonists protested. In 1773, the Americans dumped hundreds of cases of tea in Boston Harbor (commonly known as "The Boston Tea Party") to protest the English tea tax. By 1775, British soldiers were fighting Americans in Massachusetts.

John and Thomas Marshall joined the Virginia militia to fight the British. John was made lieutenant and took charge of training volunteers. John was already six feet tall and easily took command of the troops.

Facing page: "First News of the Battle of Lexington" by William Tylee Ranney.

In October 1775, the British navy took over the port in Norfolk, Virginia. In November, Virginia's governor, Lord Dunsmore, put the state under military rule. Anyone who opposed him would be labeled as a traitor. The colonists prepared to fight.

Marshall's regiment was called the Culpeper Minutemen, because they could be ready to fight at a minute's notice. Their shirts were embroidered with Patrick Henry's famous slogan, "Liberty or Death." The 350-member Culpeper Minutemen Battalion marched to Norfolk to fight the "redcoats." The British were called redcoats because their uniforms were topped with bright red coats.

The minutemen set up defenses on the outskirts of Norfolk. On December 9, the British attacked them. The inexperienced minutemen fought bravely, soon defeating 500 well-trained redcoats. Marshall's troops pushed into Norfolk, but the British navy pounded the city with cannon fire from their ships. The retreating soldiers set fires and burned the city to the ground. Although Norfolk was destroyed, the British were driven from Virginia. Not a single Culpeper Minuteman was killed.

Men dressed as American Revolutionary soldiers stand on a hillside at dusk during a reenactment of a battle.

"A Cause Most Precious"

ON JULY 4, 1776, the Continental Congress adopted the Declaration of Independence in Philadelphia, Pennsylvania. This told the British—and the world—that America was free from British rule. Later that month, John Marshall became a lieutenant in the Third Virginia Regiment of the Continental Army. Marshall wrote that he was serving "with brave men from different states who were risking life and everything valuable in a common cause believed by all to be most precious."

The Continental Army, however, was poorly equipped and poorly trained. After one victory, the rag-tag army was pounded by the British. Marshall was wounded in the hand in October 1777.

As a member of the Third Virginia Regiment of the Continental Army, John Marshall fought at the Battle of Brandywine in Pennsylvania (above). The Americans suffered defeat at the hands of superior British forces, but the battle proved that the Continental Army could fight in an organized manner on the open battlefield.

By the winter of 1777, the redcoats had conquered Philadelphia. The Continental troops were forced into the woods as British soldiers settled into the city for Christmas. The Americans set up camp in a hilly area called Valley Forge, 18 miles (29 km) northwest of Philadelphia.

With no other shelter, Continental soldiers built crude huts from twigs and mud. In a few weeks, thousands of these drafty huts covered the hills. Twelve men packed into every cabin, where they huddled around smoky fires. Icy winds blew through the walls.

Facing page: A Continental soldier stands guard at Valley Forge during the winter of 1777-78. As the under-equipped army suffered in misery, thousands lost their lives to sickness and the bitter cold.

In December, the meat ran out. Marshall and other officers lived on hickory nuts and potatoes. The soldiers ate "firecakes," an awful meal made of flour, leaves, ashes, and water, which were baked over hot stones. Disease spread through the camp, leaving two-thirds of the men too sick for duty. Marshall himself had only one shirt and a single blanket. In spite of the hardships, he remained healthy.

Marshall was made Deputy Judge Advocate at Valley Forge. This meant that he was in charge of military discipline and settling disputes between the cold, hungry soldiers. He kept up the troops' spirits by telling them entertaining stories and planning games.

Facing page: General George Washington rides among his troops at Valley Forge.

Soldier to Lawyer

MARSHALL FOUGHT, suffered, and survived two more years in the Continental Army. In December 1779, he was sent back to Virginia to recruit more soldiers. Marshall, however, got tired of waiting for Virginia lawmakers to summon more men. In May 1780, he decided to study law at the College of William and Mary in Williamsburg, Virginia.

At college, Marshall learned about the American legal system, which was based on English law. He argued mock cases in class. He joined a college honor society called Phi Beta Kappa to learn debating skills. Marshall received a license to practice law on August 28, 1780. It was signed by Virginia's governor, Thomas Jefferson.

Facing page: a profile portrait of a young John Marshall.

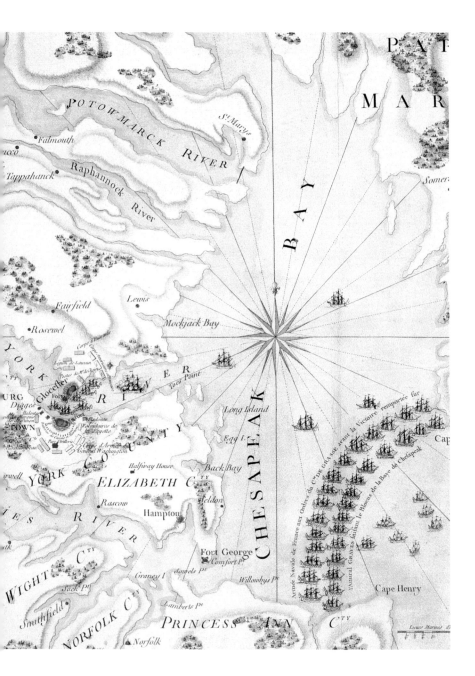

In January 1781, American traitor Benedict Arnold led British troops into Virginia. Arnold sailed up the James River to attack Virginia's new capital, Richmond. Governor Jefferson and other officials fled the city. Hearing the news, Marshall quickly rejoined the army to command a militia unit.

Marshall's troops could not keep the British from reaching Richmond. The redcoats burned the city's arsenal, warehouses, and ships before leaving. Marshall stayed in the army until February 12, 1781. By the end of that year, the Continental Army had defeated the redcoats in Yorktown, Virginia. The British army surrendered. America was a free country.

Facing page: A French map of Washington's victory over Cornwallis at the Battle of Yorktown in 1781. The battle ended years of war and won American independence.

Law and Politics

I N 1782, MARSHALL was elected to Virginia's lawmaking body, the House of Delegates. As a state lawmaker, Marshall made friends with notable patriots such as Patrick Henry, James Madison, and James Monroe. The men would gather over dinner. Talk would turn to the problems with America's first constitution, called the Articles of Confederation. Under the Articles, the states could raise taxes and control trade for themselves. This led to bitter rivalries between states. The national government could do little to control each state.

A portrait of Mary Willis Ambler.

A letter written by John Marshall to "My dearest Polly," dated August 8, 1800.

John Marshall was married to Mary Willis Ambler (whom he always referred to as "my dearest Polly") on January 3, 1783. He was 27 years old; she was 17. The two settled into a small home in Richmond, where John practiced law and attended the House of Delegates. By 1790, the Marshalls were wealthy enough to build a large home in Richmond with a dining room that could seat 32 people.

Between 1784 and 1805, the Marshalls had 10 children. Four died before they reached their teens. Polly Marshall was always frail and delicate. She suffered bouts of depression for many years and was an invalid most of her life.

Arguing for the Constitution

AS A YOUNG LAWYER, Marshall helped veteran soldiers from the Revolutionary War. The soldiers had been promised pensions and land as a reward for their service. The veterans, however, had problems getting the states to honor their wartime promises.

Marshall was a great lawyer, but he was not a graceful man. He was a careless dresser who wore his shirt untucked from his pants. He made abrupt and nervous movements and could barely hold a cup of tea without spilling it. He was described as "a slovenly dressed [man] in loose summer apparel with piercing black eyes." But he debated like "some great bird, which flounders on the earth for a while before it acquires the impetus to sustain its soaring flight."

Facing page: A portrait of John Marshall.

In spite of his sloppy manner, Marshall was a very busy lawyer. Between 1790 and 1799, he argued 113 cases before the Virginia Court of Appeals. In 1790, President George Washington asked Marshall to be the attorney general for the United States. Marshall turned the job down because the pay would not provide for his growing family.

In June 1788, Marshall was one of 168 delegates chosen to decide whether Virginia should ratify (adopt) the new United States Constitution. Most Virginians did not support the Constitution. They had done well under the Articles of Confederation and did not want to change things.

Marshall argued in favor of the Constitution. His army experience had left him disappointed with the way the states had recruited and supplied the military. He believed a strong central government was needed to settle disputes between states.

Marshall also strongly believed in a strong federal court system as provided in the Constitution. He argued, "To what quarter will you look for protection from a [violation of] the Constitution if you do not give the power to the judiciary? There is no other body which can afford such protection." The Virginia convention approved the Constitution. Marshall's speech helped swing the vote in favor of ratification.

A copy of the Constitution superimposed over the flag of the United States.

The XYZ Affair

TWO POLITICAL PARTIES emerged in American politics once the Constitution was adopted. They were called the Federalists and the Republicans. The Republicans tended to be southerners who were independent farmers. They supported the rights of the common man against the government and states' rights over federal rights. At the time, France and England were at war. Republicans such as Vice President Jefferson supported the French.

Federalists believed in a strong central government over states' rights. They were bankers, factory owners, and businessmen. These men still traded with England, so Federalists supported England in the war against France. Marshall was one of the few Federalist lawmakers in Virginia. America remained neutral in the war.

The John Marshall House, built in 1791, stands in Richmond, Virginia.

In 1796, Federalist John Adams was elected second president of the United States. By this time, French ships were attacking American trading ships bound for England. To avoid war, Adams asked Marshall to join a three-man team to negotiate peace in France. Marshall could not speak French and thought himself too clumsy to be a diplomat. But the job paid $20,000 (about $168,000 in today's money). Marshall thought he could do the job in six months. He was there for more than a year.

Negotiations with the French were very difficult. The Americans were treated badly or ignored. The French made impossible demands. Marshall was frustrated and missed his wife. President Adams reported the negotiators' slow progress to Congress.

To keep their identities secret, the French negotiating agents were called by the letters X, Y, and Z in published reports. While X, Y, and Z stalled, French ships continued to plunder American ships. The incident became known as the XYZ Affair, and turned American public opinion against the French.

The diplomats never settled any disputes with France. Nevertheless, when Marshall returned to America in 1798, he was treated as a hero. When Marshall went to Philadelphia to report to Adams, crowds turned out to cheer him. Church bells pealed, cannons thundered, and throngs of people mobbed the streets. Hundreds of senators, judges, and military men turned out to honor the diplomat.

"Cinque-tetes, or the Paris Monster." A political cartoon on the XYZ Affair shows staunch Americans resisting the threats and demands for money from Revolutionary France.

Congressman to Secretary of State

THE XYZ AFFAIR made John Marshall a national name. When he returned to Virginia he was asked to run for Congress. Marshall did not want to run. He was eager to get back to his law business. But George Washington invited Marshall to his home to persuade the lawyer to run. He convinced Marshall to put the love of his country before his need to make money. To run, Marshall had to turn down an offer from President Adams to become a Supreme Court justice.

Although he was a Federalist, Marshall disagreed with many of the party's actions in Congress. And he was not afraid to speak out against them. In a tight election, Marshall won his seat by only 108 votes. When the Sixth Congress met in 1799, it was Marshall's sad duty to announce the death of George Washington. He said, "Our Washington is no more! The Hero, the Sage, and the Patriot of America... lives now only in his great actions and in the hearts of an affectionate and afflicted people."

The Sixth Congress was marked by bitter feuding between the Republicans and the Federalists. In 1800, two days before Congress went home, President Adams named Marshall secretary of state. Marshall did not want the position. He wrote, "I never felt more doubt than on the question of accepting or declining this offer."

A view of Washington, D.C., around 1800.

Chief Justice Marshall

THE POLITICAL BATTLES of the Sixth Congress caused President Adams to be defeated in the election of 1800. Republican Thomas Jefferson was elected as the nation's third president. With only a few months left in office, Adams was determined to keep the courts in Federalist hands. When Chief Justice Oliver Ellsworth resigned due to poor health, Adams appointed the 45-year-old Marshall as chief justice. John Marshall would now serve as the head of the Supreme Court.

Facing page: Supreme Court Chief Justice John Marshall.

Marshall took over as chief justice on January 27, 1801. The Supreme Court was in bad shape. There was no place for them to meet. The court held trials in a small room in the basement of the Capitol building. The reputation of the court was as shabby as its trial room. Former chief justices had served in other offices and neglected their Supreme Court responsibilities.

Marshall began a Supreme Court tradition by staying out of politics. He refused to vote or take sides in an election. He also changed court procedures. Before he took charge, each of the six justices presented his own opinion of a case, as was done in England. (Today there are nine justices.) Marshall got the justices to support only one opinion. Those who disagreed would write dissenting opinions.

John Marshall was popular with the other members of the Court. Justice Joseph Story wrote, "I love [Marshall's] laugh, it is too hearty for an intriguer, and his good temper and unwearied patience are equally agreeable on the bench and in the study."

John Marshall sat as chief justice of the Supreme Court for 34 years. It was a record tied by only two other justices and broken by a third. One of his jobs was to read the oath of office to incoming presidents. Marshall swore in Thomas Jefferson, James Madison, James Monroe, John Quincy Adams, and Andrew Jackson.

Until 1891, members of the Supreme Court also served as circuit court judges. This meant that Marshall had to travel to hear federal cases for the Fifth Circuit Court. He went to Richmond, Virginia, in May and November. And he went to North Carolina in June and December. Marshall only spent six to ten weeks a year on the Supreme Court in Washington, D.C. However, traveling by stagecoach wore on him. Marshall often wrote to his wife complaining about bumpy roads and other hazards faced by a traveling judge.

Landmark Decisions

AS CHIEF JUSTICE, Marshall presided over several important cases. These "landmark decisions" changed the face of American government to this day.

Marshall's first important case was *Marbury vs. Madison* in 1801. It involved a man named William Marbury, who was appointed as a justice of the peace in Washington, D.C. President John Adams made the appointment late at night on his last day in office. Adams was furiously appointing 93 Federalist judges to keep the courts out of Republican hands. Jefferson was to be sworn in the next day.

Adams appointed Marbury to the post of justice of the peace, but the paperwork was lost before it was filed. When Jefferson got into office, he eliminated the position Marbury was to occupy.

Supreme Court Chief Justice John Marshall, by T. Hamilton Crawford.

Ten months later, Marbury brought a lawsuit against President Jefferson's secretary of state, James Madison, to get his commission as a judge. Marbury asked the Supreme Court for a *writ of mandamus.* The *writ of mandamus* is a court order requiring a government official to perform his or her lawful duties. These writs were to be issued in accordance with a 1789 law passed by Congress.

Although *Marbury vs. Madison* was a minor case, Marshall used it to make a landmark decision. Marshall decided that the Supreme Court could not issue a *writ of mandamus* as required by Congress. Marshall said that the Constitution did not grant the Supreme Court power to issue the writ. Congress could not force it to do so. This was the first time the Supreme Court declared an act of Congress unconstitutional.

Marshall took a simple case and made it complicated. In doing so, he claimed the Supreme Court had the right to judicial review. Judicial review allows the court to rule on the actions of state and national government. The court can decide if laws are allowed under the Constitution. This made the court independent from political parties, and therefore more fair.

There was little reaction to Marshall's reading of the Constitution. Thomas Jefferson had just doubled the size of the United States by buying the Louisiana Territories from France. The Louisiana Purchase was the main news of the day. People simply took judicial review for granted. Today, however, judicial review often comes under attack whenever the Supreme Court strikes down state or national laws.

The United States Supreme Court building in Washington, D.C.

The Trial of Aaron Burr

IN 1807, MARSHALL heard a case that was the most talked-about trial of its day. It involved former Vice President Aaron Burr, who served under President Jefferson from 1800 to 1804. In 1804, Burr shot and killed former Secretary of Treasury Alexander Hamilton in a duel in New Jersey. Burr was never convicted of the murder. Dueling was not illegal in New Jersey at the time, and it was an accepted way to settle arguments in those days. The Federalists, however, who supported Hamilton wanted to have their revenge for Burr's killing of their friend.

Burr's trial took seven months and involved 140 witnesses. It made headlines in newspapers day after day. Burr was charged with treason and conspiracy to steal western lands. His accusers said he wanted to use the land as a base for attacking Mexico, where he would build an empire.

In 1804, former Secretary of Treasury Alexander Hamilton dueled with former Vice President Aaron Burr. Hamilton was shot and killed by Burr.

Marshall did not respect the man who had shot and killed Hamilton, but the chief justice believed that Burr should have a fair trial. President Jefferson had his own grudge against Burr. The president declared Burr guilty before the trial even started. The public demanded Burr's head. Under these circumstances, Marshall warned lawyers against using "artificially excited public opinion instead of law and evidence." Like modern celebrity trials, it was difficult to find objective people to sit on the jury. Most Americans had already made up their minds as to whether Burr was innocent or guilty. Since the trial was in Richmond, Virginia, many jurors were friends and relatives of Marshall and Jefferson.

Marshall set off a furor when he ruled that Burr could be released on bail. Marshall didn't think the evidence of treason was strong enough to keep him in jail. Marshall further inflamed the public when he had dinner at a friend's house and Burr showed up. Marshall left immediately after dinner, but the incident made people question Marshall's judgment.

Former Vice President Aaron Burr (above) was found innocent of treason by Chief Justice John Marshall.

*President Thomas Jefferson (above) was furious
with John Marshall's ruling for Aaron Burr.*

Marshall caused another uproar when he ordered Jefferson to turn over personal papers. Burr needed these papers to prepare a defense. No one had ever ordered the president to do such a thing. Marshall defended the order. He said, "the uniform practice of this country has been to permit any individual, who was charged with any crime, to prepare for his defense."

The Constitution makes it difficult to convict someone for treason. The founding fathers wanted normal citizens to be free of charges from suspicious government officials. That's why the Constitution requires two people to swear they saw a person charged with treason commit an act of war against the United States.

None of the witnesses at Burr's trial saw him actually commit treason. They could swear that Burr had written letters about his plans, but since he did not carry them out, the jury said he was not guilty. The public was furious, and so was President Jefferson. By using the Constitution as his guide, Marshall agreed with the jury.

Marshall's ruling on treason was very unpopular. It lasted, however, until World War I, when Congress changed the law by calling "secret plots" to aid America's enemies "espionage" rather than treason.

Marshall the Man

MARSHALL PERSUED many projects. From 1804 to 1807, he wrote a five-volume biography about George Washington. The books were to remind people of Washington's principles of good government. In 1826, Marshall wrote a short version of the book for children.

Marshall was also outspoken on the issue of slavery. Marshall thought that America's slaves should be freed. In 1826, he wrote, "Nothing portends more calamity & mischief to the Southern States than their [reliance on the] slave population. Yet they seem to cherish the evil..." On this issue, Marshall, a southerner himself, was ahead of his time.

A statue of John Marshall, chief justice of the U.S. Supreme Court (1801-1835), outside the Philadelphia Museum of Art.

Marshall also worried about other issues dividing the North and South. In 1832, southern states rejected federal laws against taxes on exported goods. When the states refused to obey the federal government, Marshall wrote, "I yield slowly to the conviction that our Constitution cannot last. The Union has been prolonged this far by miracles."

The Trail of Tears

MARSHALL WAS ASHAMED of the way the government treated Native Americans. By the 1800s, Cherokee people were peaceful farmers in Georgia. They had their own constitution and laws. The state of Georgia wanted Cherokee lands for white farmers to grow cotton. The Cherokee, however, had signed treaties with the federal government granting them ownership of their lands.

The Cherokee asked the federal government for protection. Instead, President Andrew Jackson signed the Indian Removal Bill in 1830. The law was to force the Cherokee off their land and "remove them" to the Oklahoma Territories.

A portrait of Andrew "Old Hickory" Jackson (1767-1845), seventh president of the United States. It was Jackson who signed the Indian Removal Bill into law in 1830, forcing the Cherokee people to move to the Oklahoma Territories.

The land set aside for the Cherokee in Oklahoma was not good for farming. In 1831, the Cherokee sued the state of Georgia in the Supreme Court. The natives claimed to be members of an independent nation. Marshall ruled against the Cherokee, but he later regretted it. In another case, in 1832, Marshall wrote:

"The Cherokee Nation is a distinct community in which the laws of Georgia can have no force, and which the citizens of Georgia have no right to enter but with the assent of the Cherokees themselves, or in conformity with treaties, and with the acts of Congress."

President Jackson was outraged at Marshall's decision granting independence to the Cherokee. Jackson said, "Well, John Marshall has made his decision, now let him enforce it." The Supreme Court could not force anyone to obey its rulings. In 1838, the Cherokee were forced to march over 1,000 miles (1,609 km) to Oklahoma. The march was called the "Trail of Tears." Thousands of Cherokee died along the way.

A painting of the "Trail of Tears" by Robert Lindreaux.

The Deaths of Polly and John Marshall

BY 1831, JOHN MARSHALL had outlived many of his friends. In November of that year, the 76-year-old Marshall underwent surgery to remove kidney stones. On Christmas Day, his wife Polly died. They had been married 48 years.

At the close of the 1835 Supreme Court term, Marshall injured his spine in a stagecoach accident. The 79-year-old judge had also been suffering from liver disease. On July 6, 1835, the Chief Justice died.

The entire nation mourned the passing of John Marshall. Friend and foe alike spoke of Marshall's integrity and patriotism. His court rulings were said to be "a monument of fame far beyond the memorials of political and military glory."

A statue of Chief Justice John Marshall.

Marshall's Lasting Impact

T O THIS DAY, the Supreme Court still bases some of its decisions on Marshall's rulings. The Constitution could not cover the thousands of laws written since it was ratified, but judges like Marshall helped fill in the blanks. These rulings helped strengthen the national government.

During his 34 years on the court, Marshall ruled on 1,106 cases. Marshall's concept of judicial review has stood up to the test of time. Between 1803 and 1990, the Supreme Court rejected 125 laws passed by Congress. And during that time 1,074 state laws were found to be unconstitutional. By overturning state laws, the Supreme Court gives Americans the same justice no matter what state they live in.

Marshall's accomplishments were obvious at the time of his death, just as they are today. The Constitution has stood firmly as the supreme law of the United States. The Supreme Court is a respected and vital part of government. And it is all in place because of John Marshall, a boy born in a log cabin in Virginia's wilderness in 1755.

Artifacts from the home of Chief Justice John Marshall in Richmond, Virginia.

Timeline

Sept. 24, 1755	John Marshall born in Germantown, Virginia.
1775	Joins the Virginia militia. Is made Lieutenant of the Culpeper Minutemen.
1776-1778	Joins the Virginia Continental Line. Appointed Deputy Judge Advocate under General George Washington's command.
1780	Studies law at College of William and Mary, Williamsburg, VA. Admitted to the bar on August 28, 1780.
1782	Becomes a state lawmaker by being elected to Virginia's House of Delegates.
1783	Marries Mary Willis "Polly" Ambler.
1788	Argues for Virginia's ratification of the Constitution.
1797-1798	Special Commissioner to France to negotiate peace.
1799-1800	Elected to the Sixth Congress.
1800	Appointed Secretary of State by President John Adams.
1801	Appointed Chief Justice of the United States.
1803	Hears his first important case as Chief Justice: *Marbury vs. Madison.*
1806-1807	Hears the trial of former Vice President Aaron Burr.
1831	Hears the trial of the *Cherokee Nation vs State of Georgia.*
July 6, 1835	Serving his 34th year as Chief Justice, dies in Philadelphia, Pennsylvania.

Where on the Web?

Biographical Directory of the U. S. Congress
http://bioguide.congress.gov/scripts/
biodisplay.pl?index=M000157

The Association for the Preservation of Virginia Antiquities
http://www.apva.org/apva/john.html
http://www.apva.org/apva/mary.html

Virginia Bar Association's John Marshall Foundation
http://www.vba.org/jmfinfo.htm#title5

James Madison University
http://www.jmu.edu/madison/marbury/
johnmarshall.htm

The American Revolution
http://odur.let.rug.nl/~usa/B/jmarshall/marsh.htm

Information Please Biography of John Marshall
http://www.infoplease.com/ce6/people/
A0831958.html

Glossary

American Revolution: the war between Great Britain and its American Colonies that lasted from 1775 to 1783. America won its independence in the war.

The Colonies: the British territories that made up the first 13 states of the United States. The 13 colonies included New Hampshire, Massachusetts, Rhode Island, Connecticut, New York, New Jersey, Pennsylvania, Delaware, Maryland, Virginia, North Carolina, South Carolina, and Georgia.

Constitution: the document that spells out the principles and laws governing the United States.

Continental Army: the army that fought the British in the Revolutionary War.

Continental Congress: lawmakers who governed the 13 Colonies after they declared their independence from Great Britain.

debate: to discuss and issue for the best solution.

Declaration of Independence: the document written by Thomas Jefferson that declared America's independence from Great Britain.

Federalist: a political party that favors a strong central government over the states.

House of Representatives: a governing body elected by popular vote to rule a nation.

legislature: a group of persons with the power to make, change, or repeal laws.

militia: a group of citizens enrolled in military service during a time of emergency.

ratify: to express approval of a document such as the United States Constitution.

unconstitutional: a law that is not consistent with the United States Constitution. A law declared unconstitutional must not be enforced.

Writ of Mandamus: a court order requiring a government official to perform his or her lawful duties.

Index